Sports

T0011184

TORNADO DUNKS AND CHALK TOSSES

BASKETBALL'S MOST SIGNATURE

MOVES, CELEBRATIONS, AND MORE

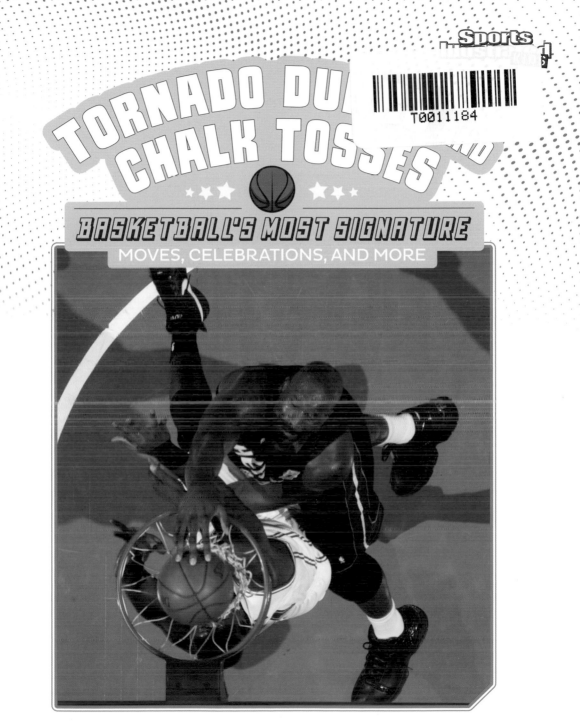

★★★★★★★★★★★★ by Steve Foxe ★★★★★★★★★★★★★★

CAPSTONE PRESS
a capstone imprint

Published by Capstone Press, an imprint of Capstone
1710 Roe Crest Drive, North Mankato, Minnesota 56003
capstonepub.com

Library of Congress Cataloging-in-Publication Data
Names: Foxe, Steve, author. Title: Tornado dunks and chalk tosses : basketball's most signature moves, celebrations, and more / by Steve Foxe.
Description: North Mankato, Minnesota : Capstone Press, [2024] | Series: Sports Illustrated Kids: signature celebrations, moves, and style | Includes bibliographical references and index. | Audience: Ages 9-11 | Audience: Grades 4-6 | Summary: "Young sports fans will discover basketball's most signature moves and celebrations in this action-packed book from Sports Illustrated Kids. Kareem Abdul-Jabbar's skyhook. LeBron James' chalk toss. Steph Curry's pull-up three-pointer. These are some of basketball's most signature moves and celebrations! In this high-interest book, discover the history behind these iconic moves and many more-from the athletes who made them famous to their history within the game. Created in collaboration with Sports Illustrated Kids, Chalk Tosses and No-Look Passes, will be a slam dunk with young readers and sports fans alike"-- Provided by publisher.
Identifiers: LCCN 2023036490 (print) | LCCN 2023036491 (ebook) | ISBN 9781669065708 (hardcover) | ISBN 9781669065654 (paperback) | ISBN 9781669065661 (pdf) | ISBN 9781669065678 (epub) | ISBN 9781669065685 (kindle edition)
Subjects: LCSH: Basketball--Miscellanea--Juvenile literature. | Basketball players--Miscellanea--Juvenile literature. Classification: LCC GV885.1 .F63 2024 (print) | LCC GV885.1 (ebook) | DDC 796.323--dc23/eng/20230814
LC record available at https://lccn.loc.gov/2023036490
LC ebook record available at https://lccn.loc.gov/2023036491

Editorial Credits
Editor: Donald Lemke; Designer: Kayla Rossow; Media Researcher: Svetlana Zhurkin; Production Specialist: Katy LaVigne

Image Credits
Getty Images: © 1986 NBAE/Dick Raphael, 20, © 2003 NBAE/Nathaniel S. Butler, 19, © 2009 NBAE/David Liam Kyle, 10, © 2011 NBAE/Shane Bevel, 16, Allsport/John Gichigi, 27, Allsport/Rick Stewart, 25, Allsport/Stephen Dunn, 7, Christian Petersen, 13, Ezra Shaw, 5, Gregory Shamus, 17, 28, Jared Wickerham, 29, Mike Powell, 8, 24, Otto Greule Jr, 11, Ronald Martinez, 12, Stacy Revere, 23, The Boston Globe/Matthew J. Lee, 15; Shutterstock: DarkPlatypus (dotted wave), back cover and throughout, onot (basketball player), 4 and throughout, sabri deniz kizil (basketball), 8 and throughout, sl vector grapy (basketball), cover, 1; Sports Illustrated: John Biever, cover, 1

TABLE OF CONTENTS

SIGNATURE BASKETBALL

Basketball is a thrilling sport. It's full of no-look passes, slam dunks, and last-second shots. But some moves and celebrations stand out from the rest. They're unique, **iconic**, and nearly **unstoppable**. They are basketball's most **signature** moves.

Dr. James Naismith invented the game of basketball in 1891. The first professional league was created just six years later.

The Golden State Warriors' Draymond Green dunks the ball in a game against the Sacramento Kings.

REACH FOR THE SKIES

Kareem Abdul-Jabbar is one of basketball's **all-time** greats. He held the National Basketball Association's (NBA) **career**-points record for more than 30 years. He scored many of those points with his amazing signature move: the skyhook.

Abdul-Jabbar performs a skyhook.

During a skyhook, Abdul-Jabbar flicks his wrist to send the ball toward the basket.

Abdul-Jabbar made the skyhook famous. This move involves leaping into the air and raising one arm to "hook" the ball toward the net. Abdul-Jabbar's height made his skyhook nearly impossible to defend. He's more than 7 feet tall, after all!

Kareem Abdul-Jabbar was so good at the skyhook that he became the top scorer in the history of the NBA with 38,387 points. LeBron James broke his record in 2023.

SLAM DUNK

Slam dunks are some of the most exciting moves in basketball.

Few players have dunked with as much power as Shaquille "Shaq" O'Neal. To perform his "black tornado" dunk, Shaq would run up to a defender and spin. Then he'd slam the ball with incredible force. Shaq broke several backboards with this signature move!

O'Neal bends the basketball rim after a signature dunk.

PULL UP & SHOW OFF

When it comes to long-distance shooting, Stephen "Steph" Curry is often called the GOAT, or Greatest of All Time. He **mastered** the pull-up three-pointer. For this move, Curry dribbles, stops, and shoots from beyond the arc. When he's on, the points add up fast!

CROSSOVER COMPARISONS

During a crossover, a player dribbles the basketball in one hand before quickly switching it to the other. This makes **opponents** think they're going to move in one direction, when they're really about to go in the other. A crossover can set up an easy chance to score.

If a player does a perfect crossover, the defender will sometimes stumble or lose balance. People call this "breaking ankles" because it looks like the defender's feet got all mixed up!

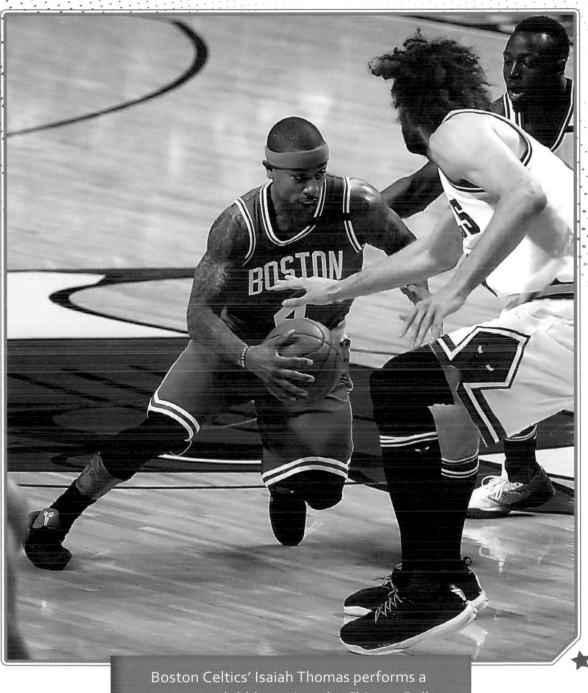

Boston Celtics' Isaiah Thomas performs a crossover dribble against the Chicago Bulls.

Sheryl Swoopes of the Women's National Basketball Association (WNBA) was famous for her crossover dribble. She could quickly change directions with the ball. She left defenders behind and created chances to score. But Swoopes wasn't the first player to make the crossover famous.

Point guard Tim Hardaway helped perfect the move in the 1990s. Some fans argue that Hardaway's crossover is the best ever.

MOVES TO SPARE

Michael Jordan is one of the greatest athletes of all time. Jordan mastered some of the trickiest moves in basketball—like the reverse layup. This move involves leaping from one side of the rim and throwing the ball underhand at the other side of the rim. It's hard to pull off—and even harder to block!

Michael Jordan won the NBA championship six times with the Chicago Bulls. His signature moves played a big part in his success.

Michael Jordan attempts a reverse layup.

The Chicago Bulls' Michael Jordan shoots a fadeaway jumper agains the Boston Celtics.

Another signature Jordan play is the fadeaway jumper, where he shoots the ball while jumping away from the net. Landing a fadeaway requires perfect timing and force.

FAMOUS FOOTWEAR

One of the biggest signs of success in basketball is a signature shoe. In 2022, Seattle Storm power forward Breanna Stewart became the first WNBA player in more than a decade to have a shoe with her name on it.

Michael Jordan's line of sneakers, called "Air Jordans," are maybe the most famous basketball shoes of all time. The first Air Jordan model, the Air Jordan 1, was introduced in 1985.

Breanna Stewart playing in her Stewie 1 sneakers in 2022.

KEEP YOUR EYES ON THE BALL

Earvin "Magic" Johnson is one the greatest point guards of all time. During his time with the Los Angeles Lakers, the team was known for a fast, flashy style of play.

Magic Johnson shoots a skyhook, which he learned from his Lakers teammate Kareem Abdul-Jabbar.

One of the secrets to Johnson's skill was the no-look pass. Players normally look at their teammates when passing the ball. But Johnson was an expert at looking his opponent straight in the eye while sending the ball flying to a teammate. The other team could never guess where he was going to pass next!

Magic Johnson was an all-star passer. He recorded an impressive total of 10,141 assists during his NBA career. This places him seventh on the all-time assists leaders list in NBA history.

CROWN THE KING

Some of basketball's most famous moves take place before the game even starts. LeBron "King" James holds the current NBA record for scoring. He is considered by many to be the best player of all time.

He's known for tossing chalk into the air before games. This **tradition** is beloved by fans all over the world.

GLOSSARY

all time (AWL-tahym)—referring to the greatest or most memorable of all time

career (kuh-REER)—a person's progress or course of action in their profession over a period of time

iconic (eye-KON-ik)—widely recognized and admired, representing a symbol or image of something

mastered (MAS-terd)—to have become skilled or proficient in a particular area or activity

opponent (uh-POH-nuhnt)—a person or team that is competing against another in a contest

signature (SIG-nuh-cher)—unique and distinctive, representing a characteristic or identifiable quality

tradition (truh-DISH-uhn)—a belief or custom passed down from generation to generation, often having cultural or historical significance

unstoppable (uhn-STAH-puh-buhl)—unable to be prevented or defeated, going on without interruption

READ MORE

Doeden, Matt. *Basketball Greats*. North Mankato, MN: Capstone, 2021.

Doeden, Matt. *Basketball's Biggest Rivalries*. North Mankato, MN: Capstone, 2023

Smith, Ellio. *Basketball's Greatest Myths and Legends*. North Mankato, MN: Capstone, 2023.

INTERNET SITES

Naismith Memorial Basketball Hall of Fame
hoophall.com

National Basketball Association
nba.com

Sports Illustrated Kids: Basketball
sikids.com/basketball

INDEX

ABOUT THE AUTHOR

Steve Foxe is the Eisner and Ringo Award-nominated author of over 75 comics and children's books including *X-Men '92: House of XCII*, *Rainbow Bridge*, *Adventure Kingdom*, and the Spider-Ham series from Scholastic. He has written for properties like Pokémon, Mario, LEGO City, Batman, Justice League, Baby Shark, and many more. He shares a birthday with NBA legend Larry Bird.